What's Left Over

Ruth Bavetta

FUTURECYCLE PRESS
www.futurecycle.org

Cover photo by Ruth Bavetta; cover and interior design by Diane Kistner; Liberation Serif text and Bodoni Sans titling

Library of Congress Control Number: 2022933986

Published by FutureCycle Press
Athens, Georgia, USA

ISBN 978-1-952593-30-7

for my husband
Leif Vogt-Nilsen
1928-2016

Contents

I

II

III

IV

I

*He cannot walk but he wants
me to bring him his shoes.*

Enough

Too many streets in this city, with their spines
drawn white, their paving black
as loss. As many as the branches
of winterbare sycamores
leading away from home. As many
as the veins that trace their course
through our bodies. Central Avenue,
broad and straight, leads directly
to the beating heart of downtown. Sunset
Drive takes you to the aging painted ladies
and their scrolls of gingerbread trim.
There's the avenue of cancer, the boulevard
of diabetes, the irregular lane following
fibrillation of the heart, the wandering
way of dementia with its bridge broken
over the river of self.

And the Rivers Shall Run into the Sea

Night leaves earlier now,
the dark bleeding away
from the horizon as day,
in its thin summer cloak,
lifts a field of sky
over slopes of wild mustard
eaten by light.

But summer is pregnant
with the raking light of fall,
a somber gold etching
the city into bright and dark.

And fall is reborn into winter
with its dark run of shadows up the valley,
faster now, faster,
relentlessly turning, relentlessly
opening the door.

Occultation

The clock never chimes seven. Sundown
seeps from heavens to horizon.

The teakettle's misplaced its song.
Succor runs dry as an empty cup.

Songbirds lost to the sky, doves, mockingbirds
and the one forever undiscovered.

The photograph of our wedding day,
colors smeared into the background trees.

The contracture of my husband's crippled fingers
as he lies sleeping in the singing heat.

Years ago, we flew to Paris, hauled our luggage
with the broken wheel around the corners of happiness.

How many days did it take to arrive here?
A grayfly crawls up the wall, slower than summer.

Almost Overnight

Hills faded from green to tawny,
wild mustard past its golden fling,
lavender of ceanothus gone.
Withering of spring,
start of summer's heat,
our onward march
to days without a shadow,
to days of hard, clear light.

In Your 86th Year

There isn't much left
of the potato salad
and there is no more roast.
Our supply of coffee beans
is running low. Library
books are overdue.
The photo of you on my desk,
so young, with such dark
wavy hair, has faded.
Morning glories, blue
in the afternoon sun,
are closing. The cherries,
so dark, so sweet, are almost gone.
Hurry, grab the last few.

The road to hell

is paved with withering white
matter, with failing
axons, myelin inflammation,
narrowing byways
of tiny arteries, synapses
slowed to a stutter,
connections that do not
connect, light
that struggles against
the river.

Where It All Is

When I wake, his eyes are open,
staring at the ceiling like lost birds.
He feels me stir, tells me he is worried.
What will I do if he dies
tomorrow? Do I have copies
of our wills? Can I even find
our money? I move closer, tell him again
that we have arranged for everything,
that I know where it all is,
that I know all the passwords.

He Asks Again

Where are my keys?

Locked in the drawer
along with yesterday, this morning,
fifteen minutes ago, inaccessible
as last year's luggage. Deadbolted,
the pin no longer fits
the housing. A combination
of numbers shifting to the past.
Hasp and staple no longer grasp
the two sections of the door
that unlocks facts and faces.
Key blank. A long shackle
catches the present only loosely.
The spring bolt no longer holds.
Pins tumble. A seized lock
no longer turns.

The Season of Forgetting

He struggles with the tangle
of winter's unnumbered days.
The delights of summer unplay
themselves, the days he watched
the field of stars, the days
he held and healed.

Friends are replaced by ghosts
with uncatchable names
who prattle on, heedless
as rain on an unshingled roof,
half-known, half-loved,
like stitches come unknit.

His brain creaks and pulls
and cannot seem to wake.
In the sky of his memory
there is only snow. Tomorrow
snow again, and silence.

How He Is

He wanders through thickets
of the past, drifting

about in an orchard of friends.
Few of them have names.

He has his books,
his magazines spilling

over the edge, and yet
he cannot find the words.

He has shrunken in the dark, in secret,
until it is no longer secret.

Finally

there is the sky
and white roses blowsy
in the afternoon sun
growing from a rotted can.
The sun is clotted with blood
as it disappears into the smog.
And then there is the sand,
washing out and returning.

Into the Dark

We sleep with only plaster
between us, yet each day lays down
another brick. Where are we
in this new world? What answers
can I give you? Each day, you walk
farther into the weeds of dementia.
Night presses against the glass.
I cannot tell you it's a dream.

Isolation

He's not an ordinary man,
few gifts now, but animal.
Like a flock of starlings,
his mind scatters toward the sun.

He tugs the blankets
to cover the absences.
The distance between us increases.
Sometimes there is no one there.

Life slides away
down the long passage.
The window closes.
The cat hides in a box.

Coming to Winter

I've spent this winter listening
for the tapping fingers of rain
on the skylight, the unexplained
electronic chirp that haunts
the kitchen, the gurgle
of pea soup on the back
burner. I've turned my ear
toward the windup groan
of the sphygmomanometer,
the sound of my husband's breath
in the night, the whine of the dog
next door who's ever hopeful for the return
of the one who won't return.

That Which Binds Us

The owl mourning
from the top of the leaning pine,
the seagull soaring in the wash
of onshore wind, the modest
brown towhee, the dark-eyed junco
in his snug black hood.

The shadow of the coyote
in the chaparral, the wide-eyed rabbit
motionless in the grass, a hesitant bark
from behind the oleander next door,
the cat on the windowsill,
the sound of a breath, fading.

A Celestial Shift

Every year the skies are higher
and the moon reels farther and farther away
to hang among stars younger than the sun.

The earth will unseal a sparkling trail
like a cauterized incision
assembled by light. The tides

will cease, lovers will fumble
for each other in the dark,
day will diminish

until it sinks into stasis.
A crow flaps onto a telephone pole.
A cockroach scuttles across the kitchen floor.

II

I love him as I love my shadow.

Happiness

If it should come,
lie down with it,
breathing *I am so glad
you're here,*

each word
a fisherman
casting letters
onto the sea.

Let it come
like a song unto grass,
the entanglement
of what is outside

and what is held within.
Hold it cupped
in your palms
like a bruised gentian.

Sommer

In Norway they have a saying,
I fjor falt sommeren på en torsdag.
Last year summer fell on a Thursday.

Summer, when the temperatures reach
a torrid 75 degrees, the balconies
of houses and apartments are festooned
with quilts hung out to air, and women
on park benches unbutton their shirts
to soak in the thin northern sun.

Summer, when the flower boxes
on every window burst with
open-throated petunias in every color
and the sun shines and shines
as if to make up for time lost
in winter's dark and cold.

Summer it was when I was there
and sailed with the love of my life
on a sailboat on the Oslo fjord,
stopping at a friend's island *hytte*
for wild raspberries and cream.

And when we docked, the sun
at midnight, at midnight, at midnight.
Oh, the midnight sun.

July Morning

Puzzle pieces of bright blue sky slip
through the branches of the magnolia.
Sun glints on its polished leaves,
turns them into patches of silver.
Across the canyon someone is building
a deck. Bang, bang, bang.

The Labrador retriever next door
barks once and is answered
by a thin, high yip several backyards away.
Wisteria shifts slightly in a breath of breeze.
A single lavender blossom floats,

spiraling down
to rest on the empty birdbath.
Beside me, my husband rolls over
and runs his fingers
along the curve of my hip.

Three-minute Love Song

Headlights
flash across the dark.
The garage door squeaks,
sticks in the middle,
shuts with a double thump.
The padlock rattles
against the wood,
the gate squeals
on its hinges,
the patio door
slides open.

This Is What My Husband Did

Drove down the hill
on winding roads
in tiny starry hours,
warm wife left in bed
while he tended another woman,
came to her masked,
in pale green shirt and pants,
to soothe flesh, pull life,

saying, *just a little while* and *push*
now, push. Forty years of babies, most living,
but not all, most perfect, but not all,
most wanted, but not all, one named for him.
Then he sutured, washed, changed,
said goodnight to the scrub nurse,

drove, frost on the windshield,
breath hanging in the air,
to let himself quietly
into the dark house and then to bed,
bringing with him cold hands
and the smell of Betadyne,
rubber gloves and soap.

Imaging the Heart

Echocardiogram: a test that delineates the deep structures
of the heart by the use of high-frequency sound waves.

The technician pulls a curtain,
tells me to get undressed,
lie on the table.
I can leave my watch on.
She sticks small sensors
on my ribs below my left breast.
Western sun and butterscotch,
smell of sage in summer.

Cardiograph: an instrument that registers graphically
the movements of the heart.

She lowers the lights,
turns on the machine.
The screen is black.
Crackerjack, Mozart, new-mown lawns.
Presses my chest with the wand,
taps the computer keys—
my heart in black and white.
Salt smell of the sea,
crisp, clean sheets.

Imaging: making or producing a likeness;
to vividly evoke.

Hilltops with views,
sprinklers on a hot sidewalk.
She touches another key.

My heart—red, juicy,
pulsing and flopping.
Sixty-seven years without stopping,
the valves fluttering,
opening and shutting.
Deer behind the shadows,
a mockingbird at midnight.

Echo: repetition by reflection of waves from a surface;
a remnant or vestige.

Early mornings blurred by fog,
waves slapping against the sand.
Tapping the keyboard again,
turning the wand, seeking.
Blue lightning streaks the screen.
Artifacts, says the technician,
pushing harder with the wand.
My husband's warm hands.

Choosing Summer

When July opens its window of sun,
we can walk the beach
in a cascade of white and green,
sea terns wheeling in a blur of blue,

or climb the hills where the remains
of the yucca's creamy bells
chime among the chaparral
and bees hum in the ceanothus.

Everything is past new, relaxing,
sliding toward the browns and tans
of August. Our pleasure is soft
and sluggish with the heat.

Making Our Bed

Shake the top sheet. It billows,
floats, settles, soft and light.
Pull here, twitch there, until
the sheet is flat and smooth.
Fluff the quilt, spread it
so we'll be warm,
plump each pillow
to cradle our heads,
tuck everything loosely
so each of us can move.
Smooth the bedspread, worn now,
its red and blue not as exciting
as they once were, but softer
and more comfortable.

This and Nothing More

Sheets thrown back
to summer. Outside
the window, bougainvillea
and morning glory
twisting together
against a blue July.
The taste
of sun-ridden hills.
Heat flows between us,
a language hidden
deep within.

The Nomenclature of Desire

The name of the lily
is the name I had before
I was born. Before white,
before red, before the moon
carved itself into one thin hair.
The name of the sea
is salt and spray
and flat blue under pale.
My lover's name is written
on my palm. The name
of the grass is always.

Love in Our Eighth and Ninth Decades

It's like lifting a violin out of its case,
a trick of the light that drives the music.
We give ourselves to these well-known melodies
as if our bodies were as they were before,
and our hearts slide into the world of sheer delight
where we tangle ourselves
in every way we're still able,
glut our mad old eyes with each other,
until everything is reduced to a single light.
Our skin glistered in sweat,
we can be beautiful again.

Division of Labor

I paid the household bills,
he wrote the check for the car.
He emptied the dishwasher, I
washed the pots. I'm the one who noticed
the dust dunes on the bookshelves.
He's the one who separated whites from colors.

I kept the Christmas and birthday lists,
bought the gifts. Wrapping paper,
ribbon, bags, boxes, postage:
that was his department.

It was an easy rhythm. One scattered,
the other picked up. A tandem
we rode without a glitch.
He programmed the clock radio,
I cracked the mysteries of the remote.

Neither of us gave a thought
to the day one of us would be alone,
either unqualified to handle our investments
or unable to turn on the sprinklers.

III

All things must disappear,
lilies, hawks, moonlight,
two shadows seen as one.

On the first day

we rolled away the hospital bed
with its squeaky wheels
and skeleton of steel, packed up
the faded green oxygen machine
with its asthmatic wheeze,
put the sheets in the washer,
dumped the adult diapers,
the alcohol wipes, the rubber gloves,
turned in the morphine
and the Ativan, threw out
the water thickener.
Folded his pajamas
one last time.

Fingerprint

There we are, my husband and me, July 2002,
squinting at the camera in the afternoon sun.
I have white hair and a bowl haircut. He is bald.
The dog is interested in the daisies behind us.

We don't know it, but it seems our brains
are equipped with mirroring neurons.
I loved him for over 40 years.
Memory is rereading a calendar of breath.

You get three days off work
after a loved one dies and then
everyone expects you to carry on.

I'm wearing wrinkled green pants, his jeans
have a hole. Time is lying on your back
watching the clouds suck and drift.
A nearby sprinkler goes *chuck-chuck-chuck.*

When someone dies, everyone in the village
moves a piece of furniture into their yard.
The next day, when the bereaved wake,
they see that everything has changed
not just for them but for everyone.

The air smells of pine trees and sun.
Long ago I spent hours making *sfogliatelle*—
the mixing, the kneading, the creation
of the fragile, multilayered shell
that holds the sweetness inside.

This Is How You Grieve

You watch haze blur
the horizon, listen to palm fronds
brush against the roof.
You make soup—broth,
onions, carrots, tomatoes,
all the vegetables languishing
in the refrigerator drawer.
You make the bed, do the wash,
try to write. When you wake at night,
a dog barks in the distance.

The Dementia Pantoum

His bed is by the window facing west.
Is this our house? he asks. Do I live here?
He does not remember when
the ambulance relayed him home.

Is this our house? Do I live here?
He turns the pages of the newspaper.
Every night since he came home
the fog creeps in without a sound.

He starts the newspaper again.
Where were we before this house?
The fog creeps in without a sound.
How long have I been like this?

Where were we before this house?
A hawk floats high above its shadow.
How long have I been like this?
Sunflowers crowd against the window.

A hawk floats high and pulls its shadow
across the garden and the lawn.
Sunflowers crowd against the window,
but there's a drought, the grass is brown.

He sees the garden and the lawn
through the window facing west.
There's a drought, the grass is brown.
He does not remember why.

Diminuendo

There are songs trapped in his head,
words and music unrelated
to the house we live in now.
Years before we became us,
he and his friend hitchhiked
the highways of victory and freedom,
France, Morocco, Algiers.
Now he wants to go home.
Again and again, he asks for his keys,
his shirt, his shoes. *Adagio, adagio,*
I tell him, this is home,
this is where you live.

Grief

fills the horizon
from north to south. Laps
the shores of the islands, Catalina
and shy San Clemente.
Urges clouds toward shore,
floats the fog along the ridge.
Drives the weight of waves
against the pier. Tangles
currents of blue and grey.
Come dark, it brings
the waterpath of the moon,
inviting me to follow.

A Fault Line in the Brain

Seagulls swerve and swoop
over the garbage dump.

We embrace the spreading
lace of the sea, or we drown

in its chill embrace.
Cracked concrete, warm

in the sun, the hose
flooding the basement.

White roses growing
in a field of weeds.

Everything is in the falx,
in the fissure

between one side
and the other.

The Bones of the Story

Afterward the house
was not the same.
Drawers held only dust
and old pennies. The lamp
over the kitchen table
flickered and burned out.
In the yard, barbed wire
clutched the hollyhocks
and hydrangeas. Emptiness
coiled in the center of the bed.

In Slant Light

In the shadow of the mountain
birds come from nowhere,
steal strands of my hair. Lizards
dart across my eyelids
as I sleep. The weight of the sun
is canted to the edge
of my days. The past persists
like a phantom limb.
Everything goes on
for as long as it takes.

Autumn Sacrifice

When I bring the pomegranates into the kitchen,
already my hands are stained with red.
The bruised globes, with their gaping wounds,
ooze crimson onto the white tiles.

The hard, dry skins resist my knife.
A slip, and my blood mingles with the fruit's.
Cooked with sugar, thickened, poured into jars,
the jelly is both sweet and bitter.

In the Desert

Released from the door of morning,
a breeze sweeps the lace of the paloverde tree
towards the ocotillo's grasping hands
and the creosote bush releases its tarry fumes.
From the canyon comes the coloratura
of the desert fox, the silence
of the white-footed mouse.
When the dry and dusty palms
sweep the curling shingles
of this desert home, we will leave
as in a dream of heat and air
and lock the door of memory.

We're finished now

with the lost keys, the dust,
the wine spilled
on the kitchen floor,
the little green house,
the poppies
on the readied bed,
our hungry mouths.

We'll never again see
the stars over the mountain,
the waterfall in the dusty canyon,
trout rising in the pond.
It's done, finished, over,
no matter where
we cast our hooks.

—based on a line by Barbara Ras

Liquefied by Light

A gap in leaden clouds develops
above a horizon full of ghosts.
It reveals the tissue of the lost,
just as the arrow of the compass
reels to find its resting place.
The imperfect past, grey as a glacier,
circles in sequence
with the hiss of waves. Light
is an echo of an echo crashing
into stars. The tides unspool themselves.
A seagull lifts and then is gone.

Only This Hour

We linger in the sheer and dappled shade of the acacia,
gaze southwest where the sun, come evening,
will lay a path of shimmer across the shifting tides.
Not for us, that cold and glittering trail,
We share only this hour of light
within light, a scene that will leave us
again in shadow, together and yet not.

Sky, Interrupted

The invisible light of lilacs floats
in waves above the garden. Sparrows

paint the roses white, dye the lilies
the color of loss. The olive tree weeps

for its leaves. Iris and peonies slouch
in the sun. After a long tomorrow,

when the hose lies unattended
and the iron gate has been repaired,

the disoriented dead will fold their hearts
and settle upon the waiting grass.

Sometimes

My heart is air. I breathe it in
and it smells of sorrow.
It is a lemon on the tree
they gave me when he died.
It is brown like his eyes
and tastes of sugar and salt.
Sometimes I am heavy
with love. Sometimes
it's just a memory.

IV

One year after he died,
his watch, still running.

What's Left Over

One and a half tubes of *smörgåskaviar,* most
of a jar of blueberry jam, a full jar of lingonberries.
Four sets of blue plaid pajamas—God forbid
I should have gotten him red. Six pairs
of reading glasses, going back
in four-year increments. Hearing aid
batteries stashed by the lamp.
Three packages of adult diapers.
Our marriage certificate.
The rest of the morphine.

Hanging On

His faded jeans, the last he ever wore,
still hang on the back of our closet door.
I could not add them to the pile
of blue plaid shirts, worn athletic shoes,
the Icelandic sweater (seldom worn
because it itched), all part of the bundle
that went to Goodwill in January of the year
he never saw. On the hook next to my robe
is the sweatshirt he bought in Madrid
almost thirty years ago. It's thin as a shadow
but unfaded. He wore it almost every day.
Paso a paso, it said, step by step.

My favorite color

is blue shading to grey
on the Pacific's wide horizon,
the orange glow of clivia
under the olive's silver
leaves, the sun
setting over Catalina.
Our first day in Paris.
Night under the midnight sun.
The taste of the sea,
the smell of the pines.
Carnations, gardenias, ginger,
petrichor.
The smell of the shirt
he left behind.

Postcard

It's dark here, and cold.
The stars have burrowed
deep into the black.
The hills are gloomy
humpbacks, the pine
sighs and shivers.
Please come,
bring sun.

Notice

the rise and fall of breath,
the heat of the cup, the cold
of the cream, the slant of light
slicing through the blinds.

The blossoms falling
from the jacaranda, the green
fading from the hills, the softness
of empty, the stillness of alone.

Job Opening

I know where these burdens came from
and how they will go on—why I lock
the front door and close the blinds;
why I forget to take out the trash
for three weeks running, dread
going to the bank, shut the windows tight
and forget to lock the slider.
Everything went by too fast,
yet at the end it wasn't fast enough.

I empty the dishwasher, write
the checks, chat with the gardener.
You were best at paying bills.
I was good with the remote.
Neither of us could sing.
I must fetch the morning paper.
No one asks for bread and jam.
The coffee filters are on the top shelf.
Come back. Be tall.

Forest Bathing

I lay in the forest last night,
I, who did not die.
The end of summer crept
through the earth beneath me.
Elderberries past their fruiting,
pinecones bare, creeper turned to fire.
Across the meadow the river
moved inexorably toward the city.
I could smell the grass and the dying
charcoal in the fire pit.
The giant leaning pine, the midnight
firs, the aspens, crowded close
to where I lay, bringing with them
the smell of dust and rot,
the onus of death and duty.

Everything

depended on fog unraveling,
taking what was left
of the weakening sun,
on the funereal green
of magnolia leaves clattering
to the bricks below, on the
only path beyond the sea.
I sent you through,
into the shimmering water.
A hawk lifted in the breeze.

Task List for the Barely Functioning

Sign the papers for the mortuary.
Hide in the bedroom while they carry him out.
Call the children who weren't there.
Tell them that at last it's over.

Hide in the bedroom when they carry him out.
Breathe deeply in the empty house.
Tell yourself at last it's over.
Put his wallet someplace safe.

Breathe deeply in the empty house.
Go to the bank to change the names.
Put his wallet someplace safe.
Try to correct the bank's mistakes.

Phone the pension to change the names.
File the last joint tax return.
Try to correct the fund's mistakes.
Look again for his receipts.

File the last joint tax return.
Check his emails and his pockets.
Look again for his receipts.
Wear his sweater when you're cold.

Check his emails and his pockets.
File the papers from the mortuary.
Wear his sweater when you're cold.
Hide in the bedroom and turn old.

Apology to My Body

I'm sorry for those cups of strong coffee
downed at all hours of the day and night.

For the countless cans of tuna fish, laced
with mayonnaise, pickles, and mercury.

For the carcinogens of spareribs
blackened over fuming coals.

I'm sorry for long lazy afternoons in a chair
by the window, gazing at the ocean,

writing poems in my head, while others
walked briskly along the edge of the surf.

For skipping the water exercises because I hated
getting dressed in the damp and noisy locker room.

For sitting on the deck at the cabin, reading
instead of hiking for a view into the distance.

For having developed a craving
for carbohydrates and fat. The bland richness

of mashed potatoes and butter. Ice cream
and cookies and pie. The sweetness

that's gone out of my life since he died.

The Clarity of Winter Air

The shore swims,
lost in the brilliance
of the sun's disappearing.
I can almost see him
in the chair by the window,
looking out to sea, not quite visible
in the diminishing light.
When asked, I say
I'm fine.

Alterations

When I return,
the house has been changed.
What was once the door
is boarded up.
Circling the building I find
only a narrow slit
near what had been
the kitchen window.
The kitchen, of course, is gone,
as is the dining room.
The stairs have been moved
to a hidden corner. Blackened blankets
are sewn over the windows.

I Can't Remember

There were only your breaths, gasping
now, the music of death flowing
through the afternoon, the sunlight
silent in the air. I held your hand
under the sheet. I can't remember
who was there. I can't remember
what I wore. I can't remember
when your hand grew cold.

Incognito

Clothespins are birds
clinging to the line in the yard.
Try to find a walking stick insect
on a dead tree. The leaf mantis
cleverly imitates, you guessed it, a leaf.
There's a bird that sings like my cell phone.
I see a discarded bicycle chain
near the trashcan, and it's a rattlesnake.
A hammer wielded in the distance barks
like a watchdog. The clink
of the icemaker is my husband,
dead for a year, seeking
a late-night snack.

Still Life with Tax Return

Paperwork from Social Security
and the Norwegian pension.

Yellow highlighter smudged with ink,
calculations on the backs of unfinished
poems, sphygmomanometer.

Thick pile of medical expenses—
doctors, prescriptions, cremation.

Records of donations—his shirts,
six pairs of pajamas, faded jeans,
his astronomy books, his favorite shoes.

Empty stapler, broken box of paperclips.
Cup of coffee grown bitter, no sugar.

Blessings

Bougainvillea bright
against the blue, hibiscus
hovering over the wall,
pyracantha quick
with berries, clouds
covering the glare
of afternoon.
Three pale stars
to measure morning.

Turning April

Sky and sea grey as the breast
of the mourning dove, mist
of morning after a starless night.

Waves wander almost silently
as clumps of seaweed strand
themselves along the beach.

I will stop looking
over my shoulder into my old life,
journey instead toward the horizon.

An early moon sends its flow
of silver onto my pillow.

Almost There

She worked her roster of duties,
stood watch instead of sleeping.
She made it past the days
she gave him sips of water from a spoon,
navigated the shoals of his failing
and regaining, weathered his sinking
through August into fall.
Now she's unloaded the ballast
of shirts and shoes he left
behind, swum through the black
of nights without solace, of dawns
that brought no light.
Her ship is nearing port. Alone
is what she's learning.
She's almost there.

Acknowledgments

Grateful acknowledgment is made to the publications in which these poems first appeared, sometimes in slightly different form.

Atticus: "Love in Our Eighth and Ninth Decades"
Blood and Thunder: "Imaging the Heart"
Dash: "This Is How You Grieve"
IthacaLit: "Enough"
Misfit Magazine: "How He Is," "Alterations," "I Can't
    Remember," "Into the Dark"
Moontide Press Poet of the Month: "Almost Overnight"
Off Course: "After Things Began to Go Wrong"
Peacock Journal: "My Favorite Color," "Everything"
Poetry East: "Three-minute Love Song"
Pulse: voices from the heart of medicine: "What's Left
    Over"
Sheila-Na-Gig: "Nomenclature of Desire," "Fragmentation"
Shotglass Journal: "Coming to Winter"
Spillway: "Autumn Sacrifice"
10x3 Plus: "And the Rivers Shall Run into the Sea"
Whale Road Review: "Self-Assembly"

"July Morning" appeared in *Twelve Los Angeles Poets* (Bombshelter Press, 2001).

About FutureCycle Press

FutureCycle Press publishes lasting English-language poetry in both print-on-demand and Kindle formats. Founded in 2007 by long-time independent editor/publishers and partners Diane Kistner and Robert S. King, the press was incorporated as a nonprofit in 2012. A number of our editors are distinguished poets and writers in their own right, and we have been actively involved in the small press movement going back to the early seventies.

Each year, we award the FutureCycle Poetry Book Prize and honorarium for the best original full-length volume of poetry we published that year. Introduced in 2013, proceeds from our Good Works projects are donated to charity. Our Selected Poems series highlights contemporary poets with a substantial body of work to their credit; with this series we strive to resurrect work that has had limited distribution and is now out of print.

We are dedicated to giving all of the authors we publish the care their work deserves, offering a catalog of the most diverse and distinguished work possible, and paying forward any earnings to fund more great books. All of our books are kept "alive" and available unless and until an author requests a title be taken out of print.

We've learned a few things about independent publishing over the years. We've also evolved a unique and resilient publishing model that allows us to focus mainly on vetting and preserving for posterity poetry collections of exceptional quality without becoming overwhelmed with bookkeeping and mailing, fundraising activities, or taxing editorial and production "bubbles." To find out more about what we are doing, come see us at futurecycle.org.

The FutureCycle Poetry Book Prize

All original poetry books published by FutureCycle Press in a given calendar year are considered for the annual FutureCycle Poetry Book Prize. This allows us to consider each submission on its own merits, outside of the context of a traditional contest. Too, the judges see the finished book, which will have benefitted from the beautiful book design and strong editorial gloss we are famous for.

The book ranked the best in judging is announced as the prize-winner in January of the subsequent year. There is no fixed monetary award; instead, the winning poet receives an honorarium of 20% of the total net royalties from all poetry books and chapbooks the press sold online in the year the winning book was published. The winner is also accorded the honor of being on the panel of judges for the next year's competition; all judges receive copies of the contending books to keep for their personal library.